THIS
BELO

Name: Age:

Favourite player:

2021/2022

My Predictions...   Actual...

The Hornets' final position:

The Hornets' top scorer:

Premier League winners:

Premier League top scorer:

FA Cup winners:

EFL Cup winners:

Contributors: Peter Rogers

A TWOCAN PUBLICATION

©2021. Published by twocan under licence from Watford Football Club.

Every effort has been made to ensure the accuracy of information within this publication but the publishers cannot be held responsible for any errors or omissions. Views expressed are those of the authors and do not necessarily represent those of the publishers or the football club. All rights reserved.

ISBN: 978-1-913362-99-7

£9

WATFORD

CONTENTS

Squad 2021/22	6
Ken Sema Poster	8
Soccer Skills · Side-Foot Pass	9
Hornets Heroes · David James	10
Soccer Search	11
Squad 2021/22	12
Classic Fantastic	14
Design a Kit	16
Ismaïla Sarr Poster	17
All Kitted Out	18
Squad 2021/22	20
Get Fit for Footy	22
Moussa Sissoko Poster	24
Soccer Skills · Dribbling	25
Guess the Club	26
Squad 2021/22	28
Goal of the Season	30
Hornets Heroes · Etienne Capoue	32
Peter Etebo Poster	33
Record Makers	34
Squad 2021/22	36
Impossible Footy Decisions	38
Emmanuel Dennis Poster	40
Hornets Heroes · Ashley Young	41
All Kitted Out	42
Squad 2021/22	44
Craig Cathcart Poster	46
Soccer Skills · Tackling	47
Odd Balls	48
Player of the Year	50
Cucho Hernández Poster	52
Colour William Troost-Ekong	53
Squad 2021/22	54
Guess Who?	56
Hornets Heroes · John Barnes	58
Tom Cleverley Poster	59
Fast Forward	60
Answers	62

1 BEN FOSTER

POSITION: Goalkeeper

DOB: 3 April 1983

COUNTRY: England

Currently closing in on a double century of appearances for the Hornets, goalkeeper Ben Foster is now in his second spell at the club.

The popular stopper first joined Watford in 2005/06 on loan from Manchester United and was a star performer in the team's 2005/06 promotion from the Championship. He then spent the following season on loan at the Vic again and joined the club as a permanent signing from West Bromwich Albion in the summer of 2018.

SQUAD
2021/22

2 JEREMY NGAKIA

POSITION: Defender

DOB: 7 September 2000

COUNTRY: England

Having joined the Hornets in August 2020, right-back Jeremy Ngakia enjoyed a memorable debut season at Vicarage Road.

Featuring in 25 Championship fixtures, 18 of which were starts, the 21-year-old made a telling contribution to the team's success. After making five Premier League appearances for his former club, West Ham United, Ngakia will now be keen to prove his worth at the top level with Watford.

3 DANNY ROSE

POSITION: Defender

DOB: 2 July 1990

COUNTRY: England

Experienced England international full-back Danny Rose linked up with the Hornets in June 2021 following the conclusion of his contract with Tottenham Hotspur.

This is now Rose's second spell at Vicarage Road having joined the club on loan from Spurs back in 2009. He made his professional debut in a Watford shirt when he appeared in a 2-1 win away to Doncaster Rovers in April 2009. With almost 300 club games under his belt and 29 England caps to his name, he is sure to be a real asset to the Hornets in their 2021/22 campaign.

WATFORD

KEN
SEMA

The side-foot pass is one of the most accurate passing techniques over shorter distances. The ability to find one of your teammates with a pass, even when under severe pressure, and retain possession of the ball is an essential factor in the way the game is played today.

SIDE-FOOT PASS

SOCCER SKILLS

EXERCISE ONE

Set up a 10 x 10m grid. In one corner there are two players and on each of the other three corners there is one player.

Player A starts with the ball. Each player must pass the ball round the square in sequence then follow their pass. A passes to B then runs after his pass and takes up B's starting position. B passes to C and follows his pass to take C's position, and so on. All of the players must control the ball then pass it with the inside of their foot.

Key Factors

1. **Non-kicking foot alongside the ball.**
2. **Pass with the inside of the foot.**
3. **Strike through the middle of the ball.**
4. **Keep your eyes on the ball and your head steady.**

EXERCISE TWO

The set up is the same as exercise one.

In this exercise the players pass the ball in sequence, A through to D, but do not follow their pass, remaining stationary.

As soon as A plays the first pass, E sets off racing around the outside of the starting point. The players must pass the ball as quickly and accurately as possible while under pressure from E, who cannot tackle but is effectively racing the ball round the square.

The same key factors apply in this exercise as in the first, but the players are required to be able to pass the ball accurately while under pressure.

Any team who can retain possession through good accurate passing will always make it very difficult for the opposition. The side-foot pass is one of the most accurate passing techniques.

DAVID JAMES

Athletic young goalkeeper David James was an FA Youth Cup winner with the Hornets before establishing himself as the club's first-choice stopper.

Born in Welwyn Garden City in 1970, James progressed through the youth ranks at Vicarage Road and made his league debut for Watford in August 1990 and his early club performances soon won him a call-up to the England U21 squad.

James was voted the club's Player of the Season in 1990/91 and after playing 89 league games for Watford, his growing reputation resulted in a £1.25M transfer to Liverpool in 1992. A Premier League legend following spells at Liverpool, Aston Villa, West Ham United, Manchester City and Portsmouth, James also won 53 caps for England.

HORNETS HEROES

HANDS

Blessed with the ability to quickly bring his hands into action to repel opposition's efforts on goal, James could always be relied upon to pull off saves and use his hands effectively to either gather the ball or push it to safety.

EYE

Always keeping a close eye on the ball, James used his sight to judge the flight of crosses and the speed of shots heading his way. Sight is such a vital part of goalkeeping particularly when quickly assessing whether to come for a ball or leave it for a defender.

VOICE

Charged with organising the defensive unit in front of him, goalkeeper James would often he heard barking instructions to his teammates. With the whole pitch in his sight, it is an important part of the goalkeeper's role to advise teammates of the dangers he can spot.

FEET

David James kept goal for Watford before the back-pass rule was introduced, however he still used his feet to great effect. His kicking could be relied upon to clear danger swiftly up-field and he would often sprint off his line to thwart attackers in a one-on-one situation.

WATFORD

```
A G F G O L D E N G O A L A A V
O C L E A N S H E E T N T X O A
D R I B B L I N G A Y H B L U C
E B P H R N R U T F F Y U R C V
A F F H I T T H E W O O D W O R K
D I L C E N S X D T V R C G R G E O T S
B M A D J P Z E U I W J F N E A D E Z M
A R P K U L I E F S B M A M P I K O S R
L Q A T A T M S D O E M T R P J P Q P A
L Y V C P O A G O I D U A A I Y T N B I
S I W U E T G T A R N V B T K A H V W N
P R C L I N I C A L F I N I S H E R N B
E R Z N S T C H X M A M A M I E N L A O
C Q E H C N S H Y O S U J G L T U E M W
I O A F O S P T E W R O D B Z A M X T K
A J I N F F O X I N T H E B O X B F E I
L K A D E A N T Y V N R K B S Q I C G C
I M G F M U G I A N T K I L L I N G R K
S X P B U H E L G L O R T N O C L L A B
T H E B E A U T I F U L G A M E S P T T
```

SOCCER SEARCH

Ball Control	Clinical Finisher	Flip Flap	Hard Man	Rainbow Kick
Bicycle Kick	Cruyff Turn	Fox in the Box	Hit the Woodwork	Skipper
Boot it	Cup-tied	Gaffer	Magic Sponge	Target Man
Brace	Dead-ball Specialist	Giant-killing	Man On	The Beautiful Game
Clean Sheet	Dribbling	Golden Goal	Nutmeg	Treble

WATFORD

SQUAD
2021/22

4 PETER ETEBO

POSITION: Midfielder

DOB: 9 November 1995

COUNTRY: Nigeria

An all-action, box-to-box midfielder, Peter Etebo joined Watford on a season-long loan from Stoke City ahead of the Hornets' 2021/22 Premier League return.

A Nigerian international, Etebo has been capped 38 times by the Super Eagles and played in all three of his countries group games at the 2018 World Cup finals in Russia. Part of his loan agreement at the Vic includes an option to buy his talent on a permanent basis.

5 WILLIAM TROOST-EKONG

POSITION: Defender

DOB: 1 September 1993

COUNTRY: Nigeria

Having plied his trade in the Netherlands, Belgium, Norway, Turkey and Italy, central defender William Troost-Ekong brings a mountain of experience to the Hornets' defensive ranks.

A Nigerian international, Troost-Ekong joined the Golden Boys in September 2020 and made 33 league appearances in last season's promotion-winning campaign. He will be keen to test himself at Premier League level in 2021/22.

6 IMRAN LOUZA

POSITION: Midfielder

DOB: 1 May 1999

COUNTRY: Morocco

Attacking midfielder Imran Louza agreed a five-year contract with Watford on 1 June 2021 as the Hornets boosted their squad ahead of the 2021/22 Premier League season.

He joined the Hornets from FC Nantes where he enjoyed a particularly impressive 2020/21 Ligue 1 campaign that saw him score seven goals in 35 outings. With supporters back in stadiums for the new season, Louza is certainly a new face Watford fans will be keen to see in action. Capped for France at U21 level, he has now committed his international future to Morocco.

There are five Harry the Hornets hiding in the crowd as fans cheer on Watford as they win the Championship Play-Offs in 2006.

Can you find him?

ANSWERS ON PAGE 62

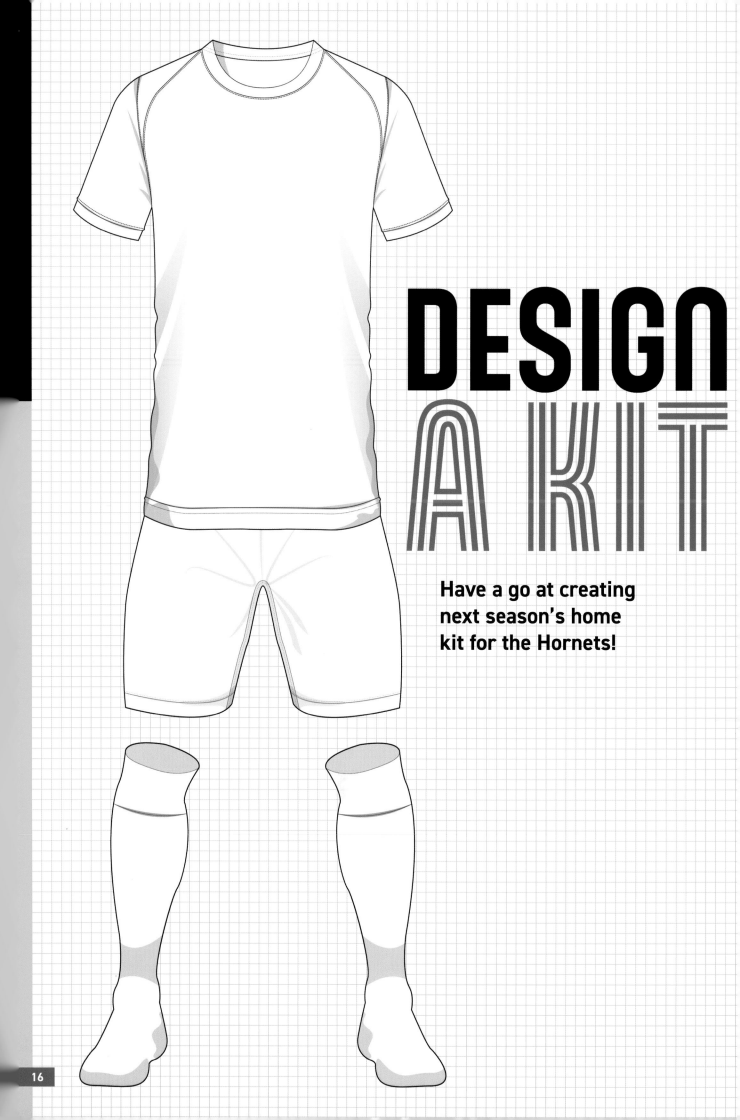

DESIGN A KIT

Have a go at creating next season's home kit for the Hornets!

ISMAÏLA
SARR

The Hornets' proud yellow, black and red colours have been a long held tradition at Vicarage Road. However, a level of excitement and anticipation still surrounds the launch of every new Watford kit.

Each and every playing strip forms its own part of the Hornets' history and supporters young and old will all have their own favourites. Let's take a look back at four of the best...

1982/83

The Hornets had a new look for their debut season in the top flight as kit manufacturer Umbro gave Graham Taylor's men a smart new strip for their first campaign among the big boys. The club also agreed a first shirt sponsorship deal with Iveco Trucks.

The all-yellow shirt had a thin black band on the front of the shoulders and a tidy v-neck collar which was predominantly red with a black and yellow trim, a theme which was also repeated on the cuffs of the sleeves. The body of the shirt housed the new sponsor's name plus the club crest and manufacturer's logo.

The red shorts had a yellow and black trim on the side and also carried the manufacturer's branding. The red socks were topped with two black bands and one yellow band.

DRESSED TO IMPRESS

The sight of this classic Watford kit brings back fond memories of the club's excellent first season in the top flight.

To say Watford were the 1982/83 season's surprise package would be something of an understatement. Against all the odds, Graham Taylor's team took Division One by storm and after beginning with an opening-day victory over Everton they never looked back. The campaign saw an 8-0 thrashing of Sunderland at the Vic en route to landing the runners-up spot and securing European football for the first time.

HE WORE IT WELL

Luther Blissett had been the catalyst for the club's rise from Division Four to Division One and he certainly had his scoring boots on in 1982/83.

Once again Blissett topped the scoring charts at Vicarage Road and his 27 league goals propelled the club to a best-ever league finish and won him international recognition with England too.

Watford partnered with French kit manufacturer Le Coq Sportif at the beginning of the 1998/99 season which saw the Hornets playing in a smart new-look strip which had a strong look to it with the shirt sleeves, shorts and socks all being predominantly red.

The shirt had a yellow chest with red sleeves and a trendy open-necked black collar. The shirt sleeves were decorated with a black and yellow patterned trim which also appeared on the side panel of the shorts. Official club sponsor CTX had their logo in the centre of the shirt with the club crest and Le Coq Sportif motif in their traditional locations.

The shorts were also decked with the club crest and manufacturer's logo. The socks were red with a large yellow top and the shin pad area of the socks was emblazoned with the kit manufacturer's logo in black.

DRESSED TO IMPRESS

Watford may have changed their playing strip for 1998/99 but their impressive on-pitch form remained very much intact as the team celebrated back-to-back promotion success.

Crowned third tier champions the previous season, Graham Taylor's side returned to the top flight in 1998/99 after securing promotion via the end-of-season Play-Offs. After ending the regulation season in fifth place, the Hornets won a thrilling penalty shoot-out against Birmingham City in the semi-final to secure a memorable day out at Wembley as they defeated Bolton Wanderers 2-0 in the final.

HE WORE IT WELL

Nick Wright opened the scoring at Wembley in the 1998/99 Play-Off final with a spectacular overhead kick to set the Hornets on course for a dramatic return to the top flight.

After Bolton had initially headed away Peter Kennedy's cross, the ball fell to Wright on the edge of the area and he dispatched a stunning acrobatic effort that gave the goalkeeper no chance. This shirt will always be associated with that game and THAT goal!

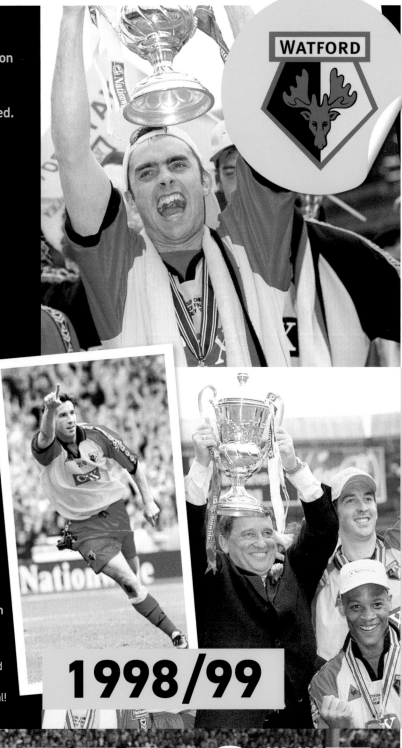

WATFORD

1998/99

ALL KITTED OUT

WATFORD

8 TOM CLEVERLEY

POSITION: Midfielder

DOB: 12 August 1989

COUNTRY: England

Having spent two loan spells at Vicarage Road, midfielder Tom Cleverley joined the Watford ranks on a permanent basis at the end of the 2016/17 campaign.

With over a dozen full England caps to his name, Cleverley brings plenty of experience to the side having previously played for Manchester United and Everton while also representing Leicester City, Wigan Athletic and Aston Villa on loan. Across his three spells at the club, he is now closing in on 150 Watford appearances.

7 JOSHUA KING

POSITION: Forward

DOB: 15 January 1992

COUNTRY: Norway

Norwegian international striker Josh King was another of Xisco Munoz's summer signings ahead of the Hornets' 2021/22 Premier League campaign.

King, who enjoyed a highly prolific spell at Premier League level with AFC Bournemouth, joined the Hornets on a two-year contract following the expiry of his deal with Premier League rivals Everton. He boasts an impressive goals-to-games ratio at international level with 17 goals in 54 appearances.

SQUAD
2021/22

10 JOÃO PEDRO

POSITION: Forward

DOB: 26 September 2001

COUNTRY: Brazil

Topped by only Ismaïla Sarr in the Watford scoring stakes in 2020/21, Brazilian forward João Pedro fired home nine Championship goals in the Hornets' promotion-winning campaign.

Spotted by Watford when still a youth player at Brazilian club Fluminense in 2018, Pedro joined up with the Hornets in December 2019. He debuted in an FA Cup tie with Tranmere in January 2020 and got his first taste of Premier League football during the Project Restart programme. Pedro celebrated his 19th birthday in style when he netted the only goal of the game to seal victory over local rivals Luton Town in last season's derby fixture at Vicarage Road.

11 ADAM MASINA

POSITION: Defender

DOB: 2 January 1994

COUNTRY: Morocco

Another important member of Watford's multi-national squad, left-back Adam Masina has seen his club form win him international recognition with the Moroccan national team.

Signed from Bologna in 2018, a physical and energetic full-back, Masina made 26 appearances in all competitions in last season's promotion-winning campaign and also netted back-to-back winning goals as the Hornets defeated Nottingham Forest and Cardiff City in March 2021.

Keeping fit and healthy is vital for all of us. So if you play footy for the school team or your local club, being fit and ready for action is sure to help you enjoy the game and perform to your very best.

For the players at Watford, showing peak levels of fitness is essential if they want to feature in Xisco Muñoz's team. Before anyone can think of pulling on the famous yellow and black shirt and taking to the pitch at Vicarage Road on a Saturday afternoon, they will have had to perform well at the training ground and to have shown the manager, his coaches and fitness staff that they are fully fit and ready for the physical challenges that await them on a matchday.

Regardless of whether training takes place at the training ground or at the stadium, the players' fitness remains an all-important factor.

Of course, time spent working on training drills and playing small-sided games will help a player's fitness, but there is lots of work undertaken just to ensure maximum levels of fitness are reached. Away from the training pitches the professional players will spend a great deal of time in the gymnasium partaking in their own personal workouts. Bikes, treadmills and weights will all form part of helping the players reach and maintain a top level of fitness.

Over the course of a week the players will take part in many warm-up and aerobic sessions and even complete yoga and pilates classes to help with core strength and general fitness. The strength and conditioning coaches at the club work tirelessly to do all they can to make sure that the Watford players you see in action on a matchday really are fighting fit for footy!

GET FIT FOR FOOTY

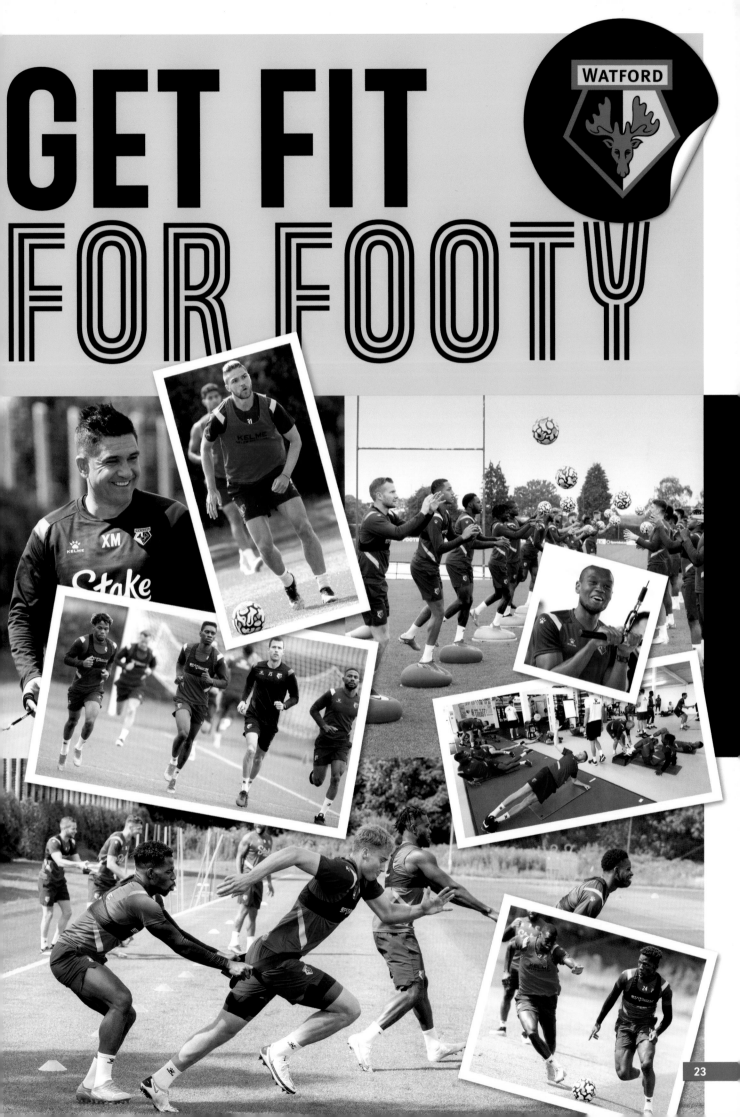

WATFORD

WATFORD

MOUSSA
SISSOKO

It has been said that dribbling is a dying art. The pace of the modern game makes it more difficult, but there are players about, even in today's lightning fast conditions, who have the confidence to keep hold of the ball and take on defenders.

DRIBBLING SOCCER SKILLS

EXERCISE ONE

As a warm-up exercise, players A and B each dribble a ball around a 20 x 10m grid, avoiding each other, but staying within the grid boundary lines.

They progress to a 'cat and mouse' race between the corners - the player with the most visits to each corner wins the race. One of the main problems in this exercise is avoiding the other player, and their ball.

EXERCISE TWO

Now for a more realistic exercise. Six players are used as shown, with three attackers and three defenders at any one time. When play starts, the players with the ball attack any of the three opposing goals, changing their target as they choose. The defenders have, simply, to stop their opposite number from scoring, but must not interfere with any other pair.

Key Factors

1. **Close control.**
2. **Quick change of direction.**
3. **Acceleration away from defender.**
4. **Feints, to wrong-foot defender.**
5. **Head up to see the whole picture.**

When the defenders win possession, they become the attackers, and go for goal themselves. This can be a very enjoyable practice, but also quite tiring.

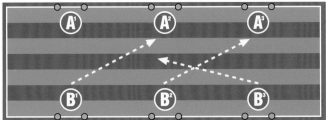

WATFORD

1 ANSWER

2 ANSWER

3 ANSWER

4 ANSWER

5 ANSWER

1932

26

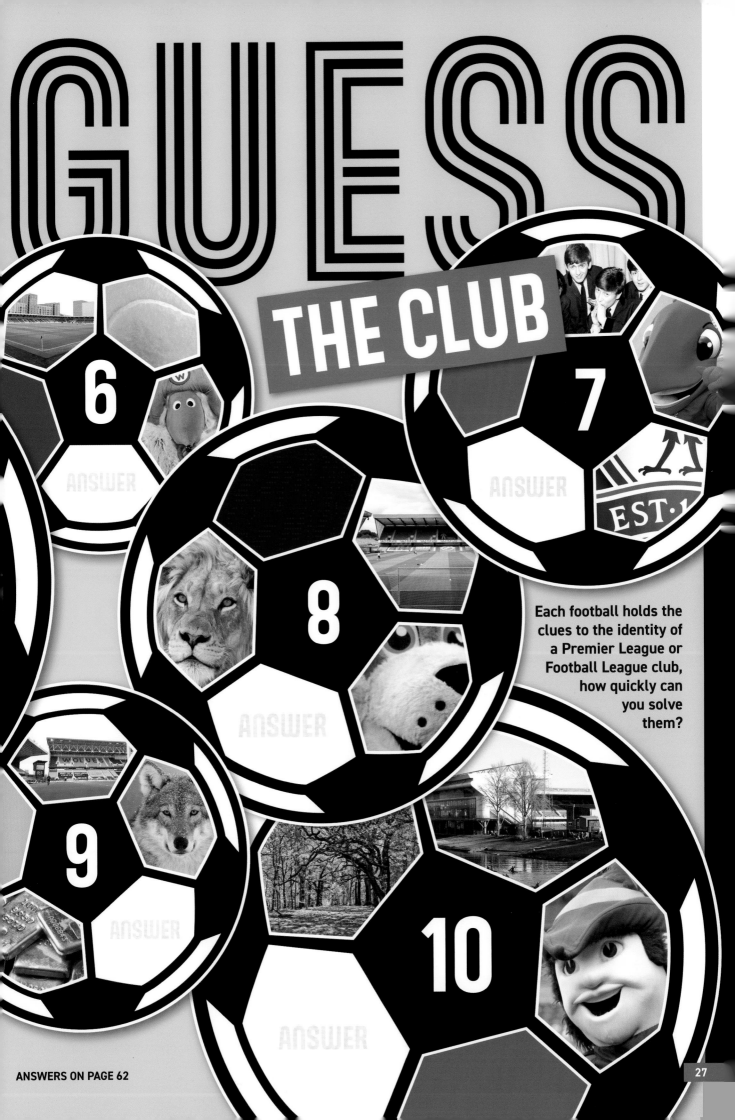

GUESS

THE CLUB

6 ANSWER

7 ANSWER
EST. 1

8 ANSWER

9 ANSWER

10 ANSWER

Each football holds the clues to the identity of a Premier League or Football League club, how quickly can you solve them?

SQUAD

2021/22

12 KEN SEMA

POSITION: Forward

DOB: 30 September 1993

COUNTRY: Sweden

With 41 Championship appearances to his name in 2020/21, nobody played in more league games for Watford than Swedish forward Ken Sema last season.

He first joined the Hornets in the summer of 2018 and netted five goals in 2020/21. Among his goal-haul last season was a brace in the 6-0 thrashing of Bristol City and what proved to be the winner in the thrilling 3-2 triumph at Blackburn Rovers. Sema's impressive club form was rewarded with a place in Sweden's Euro 2020 squad.

15 CRAIG CATHCART

POSITION: Defender

DOB: 6 February 1989

COUNTRY: Northern Ireland

Former Manchester United trainee Craig Cathcart first played for Watford in 2019 when on loan from the Old Trafford club.

After over a century of games for Blackpool, the Northern Ireland international joined the Hornets as a free agent in the summer of 2013. The central defender was a pivotal part of the team which reached the FA Cup final in 2018/19 and recorded their highest-ever points total in the Premier League. Cathcart ensured last season's promotion-winning campaign got off to the best possible start when he scored the club's first goal of the season to seal an opening-night victory over Middlesbrough.

17 ASHLEY FLETCHER

POSITION: Forward

DOB: 2 October 1995

COUNTRY: England

The Hornets swooped for Middlesbrough striker Ashley Fletcher in the summer of 2021 following the club's return to the Premier League.

Fletcher had scored 28 goals in 108 appearances at the Riverside and his arrival at Vicarage Road will certainly enhance Xisco Muñoz's attacking options as the Hornets look to establish themselves back among football's elite. A powerful forward who turned 26 in October, Fletcher agreed a two-year deal at the Vic.

16 DAN GOSLING

POSITION: Midfielder

DOB: 1 February 1990

COUNTRY: England

Former England U21 international midfielder Dan Gosling began his career with Plymouth Argyle and has played Premier League football for Everton, Newcastle United and AFC Bournemouth. He joined the Hornets in the 2021 January transfer window from the Cherries and got his Watford career off to a flying start when he debuted in the 6-0 rout of Bristol City at Vicarage Road in February 2021.

Gosling netted two goals for Watford last season, the second securing a vital win away to champions Norwich City as the Hornets closed in on the runners-up spot.

18 OZAN TUFAN

POSITION: Midfielder

DOB: 23 March 1995

COUNTRY: Turkey

Turkish international Ozan Tufan joined the Hornets in the summer of 2021 on a season-long loan from Fenerbahce with an option to make the arrangement permanent.

Tufan's career began with Bursaspor in his home country before moving on to Fenerbahce in 2015. The holding midfielder made over 150 appearances for Fenerhahce and has won more than 60 caps for his country.

GOAL
OF THE SEASON

V CARDIFF CITY · 13 MARCH 2021

All-action midfielder Nathaniel Chalobah collected the Hornets' Goal of the Season award for 2020/21 at the club's prestigious end-of-season awards event.

There were plenty of memorable strikes to choose from as the Golden Boys hammered home 63 Championship goals en route to winning promotion back to the Premier League.

However, it was 26-year-old Chalobah's strike in the 2-1 win away to Cardiff City on Saturday, 13 March 2021 that the Watford fans nailed down as being the best of the bunch.

The goal was Chalobah's second of three he grabbed in 2020/21 - the first coming against Preston North End and the third against Birmingham City. The timing of his exceptional strike against the Bluebirds coincided with him captaining the side and certainly leading by example.

The Hornets had made a tricky start to the game at the Cardiff City Stadium and fell behind after 13 minutes. However, it took Chalobah just two minutes to restore parity when he quickly moved the ball from his right foot onto his left and back again before rifling a low effort past the hosts' goalkeeper Dillon Phillips. The goal got Watford right back into the game and showcased Chalobah's close control and fierce shooting ability while under pressure from opposing players.

Not only was this a quality strike but the timing of the goal was crucial both in term of this match and the season as a whole. A last-gasp winner came from Adam Masina as the Hornets won their third game of what would become a vital six-match winning run.

In total Chalobah featured in 38 games of the club's 46-match promotion-winning campaign and made a considerable contribution to the team's success. Always known for his versatility, work-rate and fitness levels, it will be his wonder strike in Wales that he'll forever he associated with in 2020/21.

WATFORD

Highly skilful Spain international Gerard Deulofeu first joined the Hornets on loan from Barcelona in January 2018.

The tricky wide-man wasted little time in making an impression on the Vicarage Road faithful, scoring on his home debut in a memorable 4-1 Premier League victory over Chelsea. His scintillating form while on loan convinced the club to make the loan a permanent arrangement and he joined Watford as a fully-fledged Hornet in June 2018.

In February 2019, Deulofeu became the first Watford player to score a Premier League hat-trick as the Golden Boys defeated Cardiff City 5-1. A true match winner, Deulofeu will always be remembered for his incredible substitute appearance in the 2019 FA Cup semi-final. Watford were two goals down when he entered the fray at Wembley but Deulofeu scored twice in a thrilling 3-2 comeback victory as the Hornets booked their second appearance in the FA Cup final.

GERARD DEULOFEU

HORNETS HEROES

TEMPERAMENT

Often faced with robust full-backs, Gerard Deulofeu had the perfect mindset for taking on defenders. He very rarely lost concentration and always kept his cool. In the heat of any on-field duel, he kept his mind on the task in hand and more often than not came out on top in one-on-one situations.

SPEED

Not only did Gerard Deulofeu have the close control and dribbling ability to get past opponents but he also had great pace. Once past his marker, there were few defenders who could match the Watford man for speed.

EYE FOR AN OPENING

Always extremely comfortable on the ball, Deulofeu also showed great vision and awareness on the pitch. He appeared to have the perfect eye for a quick pass and a great understanding of those around him.

QUICK FEET

Operating in a wide attacking role Gerard Deulofeu had superb close control and dribbling skills plus the ability to jinx his way past opponents and into dangerous areas. Often indentified as the danger-man, Deulofeu proved to be a tricky player for opponents to get to grips with.

WATFORD

PETER
ETEBO

RECORD POINTS HAUL

Not only did the Hornets secure an instant return to the Premier League in 2020/21 but the team also set a new club record for the number of points won during a league campaign.

The Golden Boys amassed a phenomenal 91 points as they landed the runners-up spot in the Championship and with it a place in the Premier League for 2021/22. This excellent points return was achieved on the back of consistently winning matches at Vicarage Road. The side's 19 home wins and two draws from their 23-game home schedule won them 59 of their 91-point total.

Ironically the club's previous best points return also occurred during a promotion-winning campaign from the Championship - on that occasion 89 points were secured by Slavisa Jokanovic's men in 2014/15.

MOST INTERNATIONAL CAPS

Current Hornet Craig Cathcart proudly holds the record as Watford's most capped international player. As at 1 June 2021, Belfast-born Cathcart had won 58 caps for Northern Ireland of which 40 had been won since he began plying his trade at Vicarage Road in 2014.

When he won his 32nd international cap as a Watford player, he overtook the long standing club records of John Barnes (England) and Kenny Jackett (Wales) who had both won 31 caps for their respective national teams while playing club football for the Hornets.

RECORD APPEARANCE MAKER

A huge character in the rise of Watford Football Club during the late '70s and early '80s - striker Luther Blissett holds the record as the Hornets' top appearance maker.

Few could have predicted back in April 1976 when Blissett came off the bench for his debut against Barnsley at Vicarage Road that he would go on to amass a total of 503 appearances for the club.

Not only is Blissett the Hornets' record appearance maker but his 186 goals makes him the club's record goalscorer too. A number of those 186 goals were pivotal in the Hornets' rise from lower league obscurity to the top flight of the English game. Blissett amassed these records across three playing spells at Vicarage Road and he later enjoyed a successful coaching role at the club under Graham Taylor.

RECORD MAKERS

A selection of players, games, facts and figures which all shape the club's proud history.

RECORD ATTENDANCE

As we all know there are few better places to be than inside a packed Vicarage Road and helping cheer the Hornets on to victory. A world away from today's modern all-seater stadium, Vicarage Road registered its record capacity when 34,099 crammed in for an FA Cup fourth round replay match with Manchester United on Monday, 3 February 1969.

After Watford played out a notable 1-1 draw away to the then European Cup holders, the visit of United and their holy trinity of George Best, Bobby Charlton and Denis Law for the replay certainly caught the imagination in Hertfordshire. Played in sub-zero temperatures, the frozen pitch was anticipated to be a real leveler. However, a goal in each half from Law saw the high-profile visitors progress to a fifth round meeting with Birmingham City.

YOUNGEST PLAYER

Despite the plethora of young talent that continues to progress through the Watford Academy, striker Keith Mercer's 48-year record as being the club's youngest player still stands.

Mercer was just 16 years and 125 days old when he first appeared as a substitute against Tranmere Rovers at the Vic in February 1973. He was still in full-time education at the time of his debut and the club had to gain permission from his headmaster for him to feature in this Third Division fixture.

Over a 134 league game career for Watford, Lewisham-born Mercer netted 46 league goals for the club and later played for Southend United and Blackpool.

WATFORD

19 MOUSSA SISSOKO

POSITION: Midfielder

DOB: 16 August 1989

COUNTRY: France

With the 2021/22 Premier League campaign underway, the Hornets strengthened their squad with the signing of experienced France international midfielder Moussa Sissoko from Tottenham Hotspur.

A powerful box-to-box midfielder, Sissoko agreed a two-year deal at Vicarage Road after making over 200 appearances for Spurs. The midfielder knows exactly what the Premier League is all about having also previously played for Newcastle United.

21 KIKO FEMENÍA

POSITION: Defender

DOB: 2 February 1991

COUNTRY: Spain

With the ability to operate at right-back and also in a more advanced role in midfield if called upon, Kiko Femenía offers both flexibility and reliability to Watford boss Xisco Munoz.

Femenía joined the Hornets from Spanish club Alaves in 2017 having also represented the second teams of the two giant clubs of his homeland with spells at Barcelona and Real Madrid. He stood out as a top-class performer in the 2020/21 promotion-winning season and ended the campaign as runner-up in the Player of the Year voting.

23 ISMAÏLA SARR

POSITION: Defender

DOB: 25 February 1998

COUNTRY: Senegal

Speedy forward Ismaïla Sarr played a key role in Watford's immediate return to the Premier League in 2020/21.

The Senegal international scored 13 goals as the Hornets secured the runners-up spot in the Championship, featuring in 39 of the team's 46 league games, he also registered five assists for teammates. His contribution to the campaign was recognised with the Player of the Season award and also the Players' Player of the Year accolade.

SQUAD
2021/22

25 EMMANUEL DENNIS

POSITION: Forward

DOB: 15 November 1997

COUNTRY: Nigeria

With pace to burn, exciting forward Emmanuel Dennis joined Watford in June 2021 following an impressive spell with Belgian side Brugge.

A full Nigerian international, Dennis likes to operate in a central striking role and netted 29 goals in 116 appearances for Brugge. Having agreed a five-deal with the Hornets, the 23-year-old offers the team yet another attacking option in their pursuit of Premier League goals.

IMPOSSIBLE
Footy Decisions

Would you rather...

have to play the rest of your football games in 35 degree heat or a blizzard?

Would you rather...

have Ismaïla Sarr's ability to score goals or Daniel Bachmann's ability to save them?

Would you rather...

have a pause button or a rewind button for your life?

Would you rather...

have unlimited battery life on all your devices or free wifi wherever you go?

Would you rather...

run 100 laps of the pitch or complete 200 burpees?

Would you rather...

score the FA Cup final winning goal against Luton Town in your only game for Watford or play 300 games for the Hornets in League One?

Would you rather...

be remembered for a terrible footy howler or be forgotten completely?

Would you rather...

sell your best player to the Hatters for £50m or sell him abroad for £20m?

Would you rather...

have to take a penalty against Ben Foster or have João Pedro take a penalty against you?

Would you rather...

sit right at the back during a game or have the best seats in the stadium, but not be allowed to eat, drink or use the bathroom?

Would you rather...

be the star in League Two
Or a squad player
in the Premier League?

Would you rather...

Watford win the FA Cup
or England win the World Cup?

Would you rather...

your match superstition be wearing
the same socks for a season or the
same underwear for a month?

Would you rather...

**lose on television or
win with nobody watching?**

Would you rather...

have a long, average playing career or have
a short, fantastic career cut short by injury?

Would you rather...

lose to Luton Town twice
and finish top or beat them
twice and finish bottom?

Would you rather...

**clean the dressing room
toilet with your toothbrush
or the floor with your tongue?**

Would you rather...

play only five minutes
for the Hornets or win
the Premier League
with the Hatters?

Would you rather...

have to wear every shirt inside out
or every pair of pants backwards?

Would you rather...

give up your mobile phone for
a month or bathing for a month?

Would you rather...

be alone all your life or surrounded
by Luton Town supporters?

Would you rather...

play for Watford
and always lose
Or sit on the bench
and the Hornets
always win?

Would you rather...

the half-time menu got rid of pies or pop?

Would you rather...

become a legendary manager
or a legendary player?

WATFORD

EMMANUEL
DENNIS

Powerful Nigerian striker Odion Ighalo is another player to have impressed while on loan at Vicarage Road before then joining the club on a permanent basis.

Ighalo arrived at the Vic in the summer of 2014 on loan from Udinese and netted his first goal for the club in a 2-1 victory over Brentford in September. His loan move became permanent the following month and Ighalo starred in the Hornets' 2014/15 promotion-winning campaign.

After scoring 20 goals at Championship level in his first season at the club, including a second-half four-goal haul in the 7-2 rout of Blackpool, Ighalo then marked his Premier League debut with a goal in the opening-day 2-2 draw with Everton at Goodison Park. He went on to score 15 Premier League goals as the club successfully maintained their Premier League status in 2015/16.

ODION IGHALO

HORNETS HEROES

HEADERS

A number of Odion Ighalo's 39 Watford goals came from headers. A real threat in the air, Ighalo had the power to out-jump defenders and then use his head to direct the ball past the 'keeper and into the net. Once the ball was in and around the six-yard box and in the air there was always a good chance he would head it home.

MOVEMENT

Often forming the focal point of the attack alongside Troy Deeney, Ighalo could be relied upon to use his pace to latch on to Deeney's flick-ons. He was also an intelligent and willing runner who would use his movement to open up spaces in the opposition's back-line.

CLOSE CONTROL

Blessed with a strong physical frame, Odion Ighalo would happily play with his back to goal and take the ball on his chest. Benefitting from good close control and dribbling skills, the Nigerian was always comfortable on the ball and willing to receive the ball from teammates in tight situations.

GOALS

Odion Ighalo boasted a highly impressive strike-rate in his Watford career with 39 goals in 99 games for the club. With the ability to take shots first time or at the end of a powerful surging run - when Ighalo took aim he had a great knack of making sure he hit the target.

2005/06

Produced by Diadora, the Watford home shirt for the 2005/06 season continued the theme of the previous two seasons with the club crest, sponsor's logo and manufacturer's name all positioned in the centre of the shirt.

The yellow shirts for 2005/06 were enhanced by a red and black panel running from the collar down to the armpit and a stylish pattern added to both shoulder panels.

The plain black shorts were complimented by a small red and yellow panel on one side and the manufacturer's name on the opposite side. The black socks carried both the manufacturer's name and branding plus maintained the yellow and red themed side panel from the shorts on one of the socks.

DRESSED TO IMPRESS

In what was new boss Aidy Boothroyd's first full season in charge at the Vic, the Golden Boys enjoyed an excellent 2005/06 Championship campaign that ended with promotion to the Premier League via the end-of-season Play-Offs.

Tipped by many for relegation before a ball was kicked, Boothroyd's team certainly proved the doubters wrong and ended the season third in the table. Despite missing out on the automatic promotion places, the side held their nerve to overcome Crystal Palace in the Play-Off semi-final and book a date with Leeds United in the final at Cardiff's Millennium Stadium. An impressive 3-0 victory in the final provided Watford fans with one of the greatest days in the club's history.

HE WORE IT WELL

Scotland international Malky Mackay helped provide the defensive rock that the club's 2005/06 success was built upon.

The powerful central defender had previously won promotion in the past two seasons with Norwich City and West Ham United and his experience certainly proved to be a vital ingredient as the Hornets closed in on the Premier League.

The club's 2015/16 home shirt certainly took on a whole new look with manufacturer Puma producing a yellow shirt dominated by black horizontal stripes which started off as pinstripes at the top and got thicker as they worked their way down to the bottom of the shirt.

With a black v-neck collar the shirt also carried a black panel across the sleeves. The Puma motif was displayed on both sleeves and also on the front of the shirt. The club's crest and sponsor's logo were also present on the chest area.

The shorts and socks were black with a yellow trim, with the shorts carrying the club crest and Puma logo. The manufacturer's logo was also shown in yellow on the socks.

DRESSED TO IMPRESS

Under the management of Quique Sanchez Flores, Watford comfortably retained their Premier League status with an excellent 13th-placed finish following their promotion from the Championship the previous season.

A superb spell of form in late November and early December saw the Hornets win four back-to-back Premier League games and secure 12 of their 45-point total. With confidence flowing through the squad, Watford were also FA Cup semi-finalists in 2015/16.

HE WORE IT WELL

Strutting his stuff in the Hornets' new-look kit, striker Troy Deeney was once again the focal point of the Watford attack in this memorable Premier League campaign and his 13 goals proved vital to the club's success.

Deeney formed an impressive strike partnership with Odion Ighalo that often proved too hot to handle for opposition defences.

2015/16

ALL KITTED OUT

43

WATFORD

26 DANIEL BACHMANN

POSITION: Goalkeeper

DOB: 9 July 1994

COUNTRY: Austria

Patience has certainly been the key for goalkeeper Daniel Bachmann having initially joined the Hornets in the summer of 2017.

Signing from Stoke City, the 6ft 3ins Austrian spent 2018/19 on loan at Kilmarnock and had to wait until January 2021 for his first league start with the Hornets. However, he grasped the opportunity to impress new boss Xisco Munoz and made the goalkeeper's spot his own for the remainder of the promotion-winning campaign. His excellent club form was rewarded with a full international debut against England in June 2021 and he was first-choice 'keeper for Austria during the Euro 2020 finals.

27 CHRISTIAN KABASELE

POSITION: Defender

DOB: 24 February 1991

COUNTRY: Belgium

Central defender Christian Kabasele has made over a century of first-team appearances in a Watford shirt having arrived from Genk in the summer of 2016.

A full Belgian international, Kabasele has twice been named the club's Community Ambassador in recognition of his work representing the club in the local area. On the pitch he made 20 appearances in the 2020/21 promotion success.

SQUAD
2021/22

POSITION: Forward

DOB: 20 April 1999

COUNTRY: Colombia

Having spent the first four seasons of his Watford career on loan in Spain, Cucho Hernández marked his Watford debut in some style as he scored a stunning goal in the Hornets' 3-2 opening-day Premier League victory over Aston Villa in August 2021.

The Colombian adds an exciting and attacking flair to the Hornets' front line and looks like being a real crowd favourite at the Vic.

CRAIG
CATHCART

One of a player's greatest assets is the ability to win the ball. The following exercise can be used to improve a player's tackling abilities.

TACKLING

SOCCER SKILLS

EXERCISE

Set up a 10m x 20m grid.

In this two-on-two exercise, the aim of the game is to score a goal by taking the ball past the two opposing defenders, to the end line, and stand on the ball. The defenders just have to stop them.

As well as producing plenty of opportunities for the defenders to tackle, this session will test the defenders' abilities to work together, and communicate.

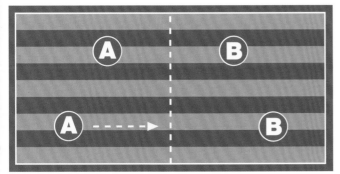

Key Factors

1. **Be patient - do not dive in.**

2. **Stay on your feet if possible.**

3. **Time the tackle with bodyweight behind it.**

4. **Be determined to win it.**

The reason that great players win so many tackles is not just because they know how to tackle and have good technique, it is because they have big hearts and are determined to win their challenges on the pitch.

ODD BALLS

Three of the four pictures in each football represent a Premier League or Football League club, can you figure out the football club as well as the odd one out?

1

- C
- B
- D
- A

ANSWER

2

- B
- A
- C
- D
- 1898

ANSWER

3

- C
- B
- A
- D

ANSWER

4

- C — FOOTBALL CLUB
- B
- D
- A

ANSWER

5

- B
- A
- C
- D

ANSWER

ANSWERS ON PAGE 62

WATFORD

6
C
B
A
D
1905

7
B
C
A
D

8
B
A
C
D

10
B
A
C
ANSWER
D

9
A
B
ANSWER
D
C
FOOTBALL CLUB

PLAYER OF THE YEAR

ISMAÏLA SARR

Flying wide man Ismaïla Sarr enjoyed a double success at the Hornets' end-of-season awards event when he was presented with both the Graham Taylor Player of the Season award and also the Players' Player of the Year award.

The Senegal international scored 13 goals as the Hornets secured the runners-up spot in the Championship and with it an immediate return to the Premier League. Sarr featured in 39 of Watford's 46 league games and on top of his 13 goals, he also registered five assists for teammates. The fact that Sarr was the most fouled player in the division proved just how tricky it was for opposition teams to deal with the threat he presented.

Fittingly, it was Sarr who netted the goal that ultimately sealed the team's promotion when they defeated Millwall 1-0 at the Vic on 24 April.

When it came to voting for their Player of the Season, the Watford faithful had little doubt as to whom their star performer had been and Sarr was presented with the award by Honorary Life-President Sir Elton John CBE. Sarr landed the prestigious award following a supporter vote which saw full-back Kiko Femenía as runner-up and central defender Francisco Sierralta in third place.

Throughout the 2020/21 campaign Sarr's teammates would sing the praises of Watford's record signing, who has played more minutes than anyone in the squad yet never seems to burn out, so it was no surprise when he landed the Players' Player of the Season title too.

YOUNG PLAYER OF THE YEAR

JOÃO PEDRO

Exciting Brazilian forward João Pedro capped off a memorable first full season at Vicarage Road when he was voted the club's Young Player of the Season for 2020/21.

After joining Watford in the January 2020 transfer window, Pedro really came of age during the 2020/21 promotion-winning campaign. He netted nine goals in 38 league appearances, including a sensational winner away to Derby County in October 2020.

Pedro soon won the hearts of the Watford fans when he scored the only goal of the game to secure local bragging rights with a 1-0 win over arch-rivals Luton Town in what was just the second home game of the campaign.

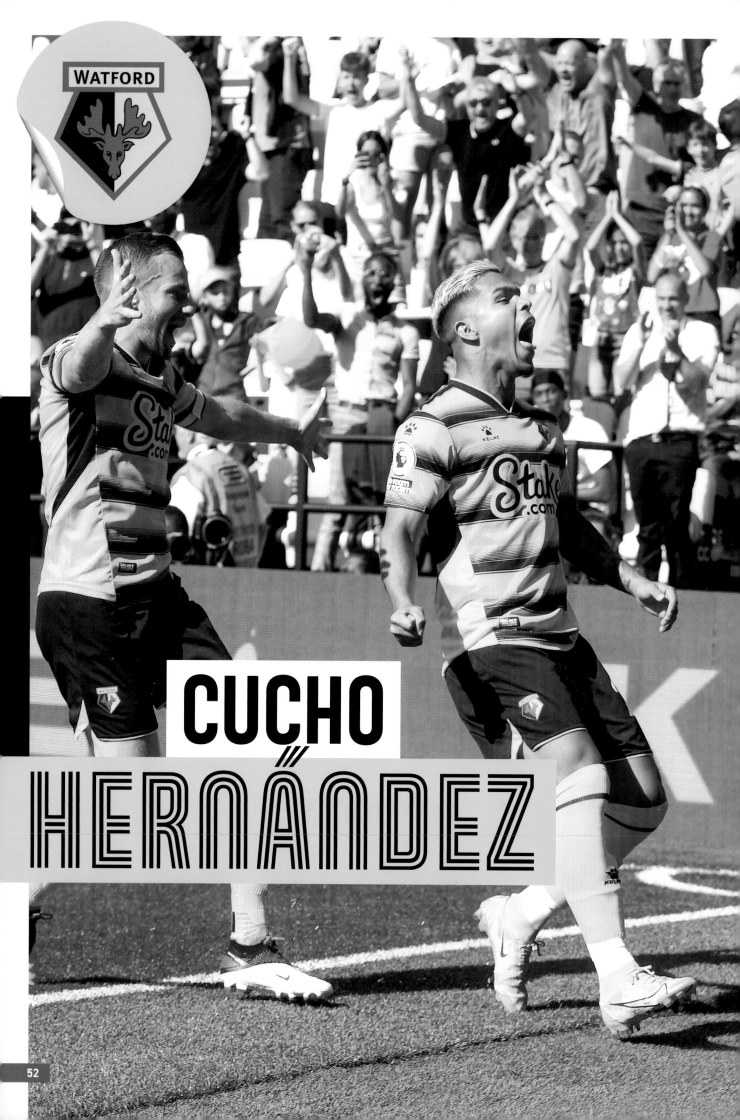

WATFORD

CUCHO
HERNÁNDEZ

COLOUR
WILLIAM
TROOST-EKONG

WATFORD

31 FRANCISCO SIERRALTA

POSITION: Defender

DOB: 6 May 1997

COUNTRY: Chile

A strong and mobile central defender, Francisco Sierralta enjoyed an impressive debut season at Vicarage Road in 2020/21.

After joining the club from Udinese in September 2020, the 6ft 4in Chilean international went on to start 24 Championship fixtures as Watford secured an instant return to the top flight. He added his name to the goalscoring charts when he opened the scoring in March's 4-1 win at Rotherham. Such was the impression he made on the Watford fans, Sierralta ended the campaign third in the Player of the Season vote.

33 JURAJ KUCKA

POSITION: Midfielder

DOB: 26 February 1987

COUNTRY: Slovakia

Juraj Kucka joined Watford from Italian side Parma Calcio in August 2021.

The Slovakia international arrived at Vicarage Road with more than a decade of experience playing at a high level, having turned out for AC Milan, Genoa and Trabzonspor. With the ability to operate as a holding midfielder or in a more advanced role, Kucka made his Hornets' debut in the opening-day victory over Aston Villa.

SQUAD
2021/22

34 KWADWO BAAH

POSITION: Forward

DOB: 27 January 2003

COUNTRY: England

Kwadwo Baah joined the Hornets from Rochdale in May 2021 and agreed a five-year contract at Vicarage Road.

Capable of playing as a central forward or on either wing, the highly-rated youngster recorded three goals and two assists in 13 League One games for Dale in 2020/21. Born in Germany to Ghanaian parents, Baah has already been capped at U18 level by England.

35 ROB ELLIOT

POSITION: Goalkeeper

DOB: 30 April 1986

COUNTRY: Republic of Ireland

Rob Elliot joined Watford in the January 2021 transfer window and adds another level of depth and competition to the club's goalkeeping department.

A full Republic of Ireland international with Premier League experience, Elliot began his career at Charlton Athletic before taking in a lengthy spell with Newcastle United. It was from the Magpies that he joined the Hornets.

WATFORD

1. WHO AM I?

I was born
in Scotland in 1957

I joined Watford from
Cambridge United

I scored the goal that took
the Hornets to Wembley
for the first time

While at Vicarage Road
I formed part of a prolific
strike partnership

After leaving Watford
I joined Newcastle United

3. WHO AM I?

I was born in
Sunderland in 1966

I was handed my
Watford debut by
Graham Taylor

I made a total
of 472 appearances
for the Hornets

In October 1993
I netted a hat-trick
in a 4-3 victory over
Bolton Wanderers

I was voted the club's
Player of the Season
in 1993/94

GUESS WHO

2. WHO AM I?

I was born in
Stevenage in 1985

My middle name
is Simon

I was handed my
Watford debut
by Ray Lewington

I helped the
Hornets to promotion
in 2005/06

I left Vicarage Road
in a big-money move
in January 2007

I joined the Hornets on loan from Barcelona in 2018

I completed a permanent move to Watford ahead of the 2018/19 season

Prior to joining Watford I had experienced the English game while at Everton

In February 2019 I became the first Watford player to score a Premier League hat-trick

My finest hour for the Hornets saw me score twice in the 2019 FA Cup semi-final victory over Wolves

4. WHO AM I?

I first joined Watford on loan

I made my Hornets' debut in a League Cup tie

I once scored four goals in a game at Vicarage Road

I marked my Premier League debut for Watford with a goal against Everton

I set Watford on their way to an FA Cup semi-final with the first goal in a quarter-final victory over Arsenal

5. WHO AM I?

6. WHO AM I?

I was aged just 17 when I broke into the Watford first team

I made my Hornets' debut against Oldham Athletic

My first Watford goal came against Barnsley

I played in the 1984 FA Cup final

I was first capped by England while plying my trade at Vicarage Road

ANSWERS ON PAGE 62

A top performer for the Hornets in the golden era under Graham Taylor in the 1980s, winger John Barnes made a lasting impression during his time at Vicarage Road.

Barnes made his debut in 1981 and went on to play in 36 Second Division fixtures and score 13 goals as Watford celebrated a historic promotion to the First Division for the first time in the club's history.

He played a vital role in the Watford team that secured the runners-up spot in the top flight in 1982/83 and was an FA Cup finalist with the Hornets in 1984. Barnes made 296 appearances for the cub and scored 85 goals before enjoying great success with Liverpool and England.

JOHN BARNES

HORNETS HEROES

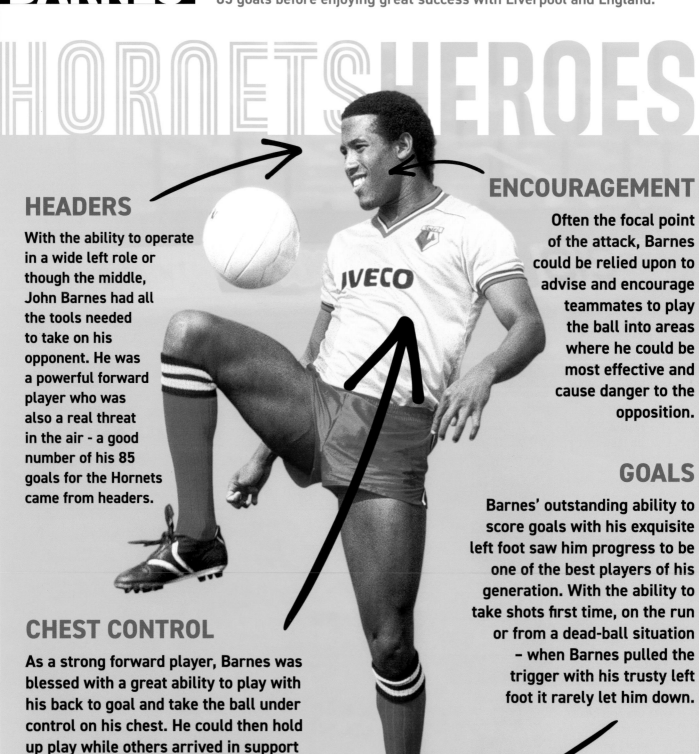

HEADERS

With the ability to operate in a wide left role or though the middle, John Barnes had all the tools needed to take on his opponent. He was a powerful forward player who was also a real threat in the air - a good number of his 85 goals for the Hornets came from headers.

ENCOURAGEMENT

Often the focal point of the attack, Barnes could be relied upon to advise and encourage teammates to play the ball into areas where he could be most effective and cause danger to the opposition.

GOALS

Barnes' outstanding ability to score goals with his exquisite left foot saw him progress to be one of the best players of his generation. With the ability to take shots first time, on the run or from a dead-ball situation – when Barnes pulled the trigger with his trusty left foot it rarely let him down.

CHEST CONTROL

As a strong forward player, Barnes was blessed with a great ability to play with his back to goal and take the ball under control on his chest. He could then hold up play while others arrived in support or lay the ball off to a teammate.

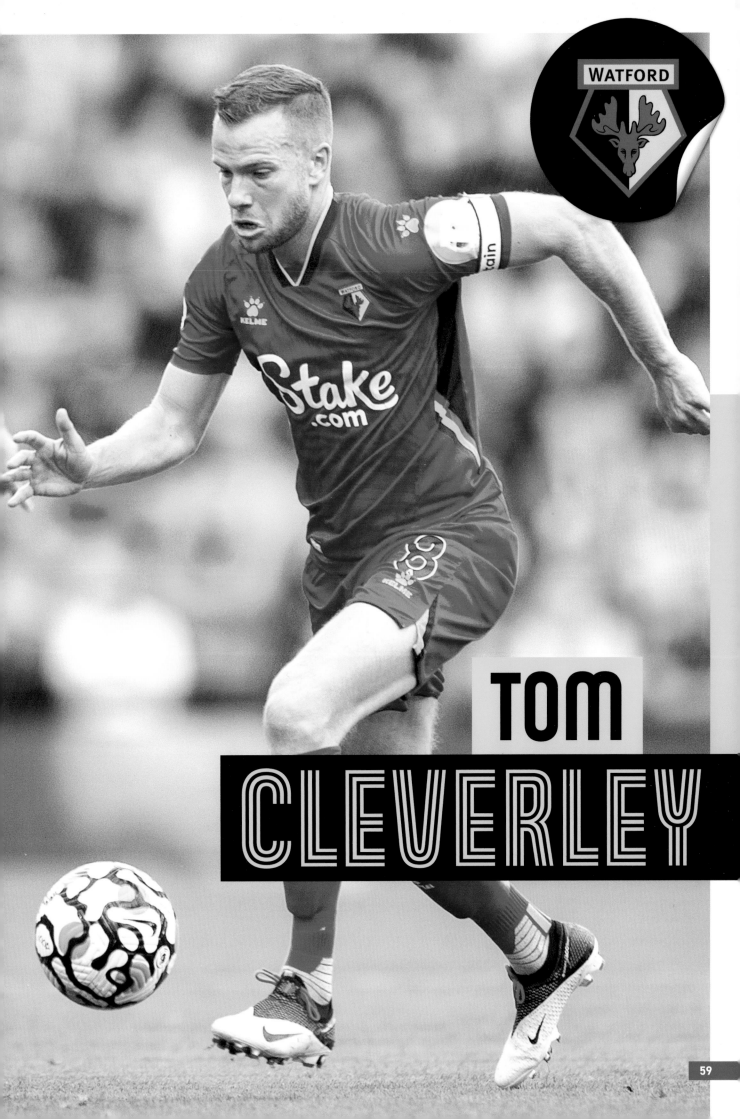

WATFORD

TOM
CLEVERLEY

FAST FORWARD »

Do your predictions for 2021/22 match our own?...

PREMIER LEAGUE TOP SCORER

Anthony Martial

PREMIER LEAGUE WINNERS

Manchester United

PREMIER LEAGUE RUNNERS-UP

Chelsea

FA CUP WINNERS

Watford

FA CUP RUNNERS-UP

Leeds United

LEAGUE CUP WINNERS

Arsenal

LEAGUE CUP RUNNERS-UP

Leicester City

CHAMPIONSHIP WINNERS
Fulham

CHAMPIONSHIP RUNNERS-UP
Derby County

CHAMPIONSHIP PLAY-OFF WINNERS
Reading

CHAMPIONSHIP TOP SCORER
Ivan Cavaleiro

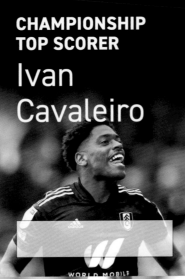

HORNETS TOP SCORER
Emmanuel Dennis

CHAMPIONS LEAGUE WINNERS
Barcelona

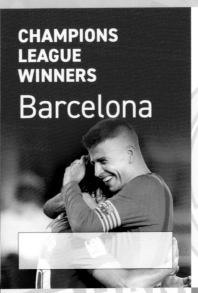

CHAMPIONS LEAGUE RUNNERS-UP
Real Madrid

HORNETS PLAYER OF THE YEAR
Cucho Hernández

EUROPA LEAGUE WINNERS
West Ham United

EUROPA LEAGUE RUNNERS-UP
Lazio

ANSWERS

PAGE 11
SOCCER SEARCH

Bicycle Kick.

PAGE 14
CLASSIC FANTASTIC

PAGE 26
GUESS THE CLUB

1. Newcastle United. 2. Wigan Athletic. 3. Leeds United.
4. Charlton Athletic. 5. Coventry City. 6. AFC Wimbledon.
7. Liverpool. 8. Millwall. 9. Wolverhampton Wanderers.
10. Nottingham Forest.

PAGE 48
ODD BALLS

1. Sunderland, C. 2. Portsmouth, C. 3. Arsenal, B.
4. Crewe Alexandra, A. 5. Queens Park Rangers, C.
6. Crystal Palace, B. 7. Tottenham Hotspur, B.
8. Reading, B. 9. Birmingham City, C.
10. West Ham United, D

PAGE 56
GUESS WHO?

1. George Reilly. 2. Ashley Young. 3. Gary Porter.
4. Gerard Deulofeu. 5. Odion Ighalo. 6. John Barnes.